Plan for Success

Plan for Success

An Organizing Guide
for Prehealth Professions Students

Charles E. Kozoll, Ph.D

Published by:
The National Association of Advisors
for the Health Professions, Inc.
P.O. Box 5017-A
Champaign, Illinois 61820-9017

Printed in Saline, Michigan

Published by:
The National Association of Advisors for the Health Professions, Inc.

Library of Congress Cataloging in Publication Data
Kozoll, Charles E.
    Plan for Success.

        1. Premedical education. 2. Medicine–Vocational guidance. 3.
College students–Time management. 4. Time management. I. Title.
ISBN 0-911899-03-0

Contents

Acknowledgements

This publication is built upon the insights and approaches used by many pre-health profession advisors. Julian Frankenberg and Nancy Williams of NAAHP provided guidance, management, and support as the booklet was prepared. Editorial comments by Norman Sansing and Tony Smulders were particularly valuable.

Editing by Olga Murphy added a great deal to the text's organization and overall clarity. Marlynna Schaefer diligently inputted many revisions with unfading cheerfulness.

I am grateful to the many undergraduate students, particularly those at the University of Illinois at Urbana-Champaign, who shared approaches to academic success as well as the joys associated with accomplishment and excellence.

Plan for Success

Is it your dream to become a physician? a nurse? a pharmacist? a medical technologist? If you dream of becoming a professional in one of these highly regarded and growing health career fields– or in another, including dentistry and dental hygiene, occupational and respiratory therapy, and radiological, surgical, and veterinary technology, among others– then you have a dream that many bright, ambitious young people share. Some of those dreamers will realize their dreams; many others will not. It's easy to dream and so much harder to do. Dreams don't turn themselves into reality; someone has to *make* them happen and that someone is not a dreamer, but a doer.

Of course, every one of us is both a dreamer and a doer. The dreamer in us sets our goals; the doer in us reaches them. By selecting a health professions career, you have identified an important set of goals. Reaching these goals won't be easy because of challenges you are about to face. Approaching them realistically is critical to your academic success and to your overall preparation for a health professions career.

Many academic counselors emphasize that the first six weeks of your first semester are critical. For in that time, along with many other responsibilities, you must concentrate on developing sound organizing methods and on learning how much time and energy is needed to handle your courses. With a strong organizing plan, you will be better prepared to handle the unexpected and be able to overcome obstacles that may deter you from reaching your goal. If you do fall behind, you can still develop sound study skills but will have the extra burdens of developing these along with catching up on your workload.

With your dream of a career in any of the health professions fields, you have the beginning motivation. By following the guidelines presented here, you can channel that motivation, experience regular academic achievement, and enjoy the exhilaration of growth toward your chosen career. These guidelines have benefited many successful students, and they can benefit you as well. By being a doer, like the student examples used in this booklet, you too can reach your goals. Both Ellen and Jane had the motivation to follow the guidelines presented here; John did not.

Ellen Kerwin, Jane Delio, and John Chandler are a composite of many students who were interviewed in preparation of this booklet and will be described in the next few chapters.

Many of the suggested guidelines will already be familiar to you. You may currently rely on some of them now. Like Ellen and Jane, you must realize that in a competitive college environment these guidelines will become essential in order to achieve and to succeed.

Remember too that success has different definitions. Excellent grades and a high score on an admissions test is one part of the definition. That combination might get you into a professional school, but that is not all you need. You must master the material that will build a foundation for your continuing studies. (What is the use of gaining admission if you can't get out?) You need to be able to control the pressure in a competitive college or university. (You don't get to be a gastroenterologist by giving yourself an ulcer.) And you need to enjoy life beyond the classroom, because those who care and feel for others should know how to relax and to relieve stress likely to be faced throughout their lives.

You can have this kind of success if:

- Your motivation for becoming a physician, nurse, therapist or other health professional is clear, meaningful, and a driving force behind each day's efforts.
- Your semester or quarter goals are carefully designed and directed toward habitual academic excellence.
- You learn to concentrate and focus on a task, not allowing yourself to be easily distracted.
- Your time is planned around a specific set of priorities.
- You develop habits that make concentration a central part of your study routine.
- You take time to prepare for classes.
- You build in time to relax and to enjoy life.
- You know how to anticipate and to relieve pressure.

Developing these abilities will require discipline and support. Professional staff at your college or university are ready to assist you. During the first six weeks and thereafter, learn to rely on help from academic as well as your health professions advisors, residence hall counselors, and faculty members. A list of offices that are found on most campuses is provided in Appendix 2.

By knowing both your goals and how to achieve them, you will be able to do the following:

- Clarify your motivation to enter the health professions field and make it the force behind effective planning, behind wise use of time each day, behind focused study, and behind intelligent management of pressure.
- Plan for academic excellence each semester or quarter using a routine

that emphasizes continuous preparation for every course, regular rather than last minute study, and true mastery of material.

- Establish and maintain limits on how much you attempt beyond your studies, especially if you have to work while in school or have other obligations.
- Concentrate at every study session so that you are able to avoid self-induced or external distractions, and end each session with a strong sense of accomplishment.
- Identify and become committed to a few logical time management, study, and pressure control techniques.

Even with strong organization, your life won't be bump and jam free. The unexpected will make days difficult. Research on those hearty personalities who achieve and who handle pressure emphasizes that learning from those bumps and jams is important, as is recognizing they will happen to all of us. By developing a sound organization plan and by learning to anticipate difficulties, you will acquire the ability to handle the unexpected and benefit throughout your career.

Some students, like Ellen Kerwin and Jane Delio, come to college already equipped with clear motivation, strong study skills, and time management abilities. They were fortunate in having guidance from parents, teachers, and coaches during high school. John Chandler, however, wasn't as fortunate, and he almost found himself squeezed out of success.

This booklet is written for all the John Chandler's whose potential can be fully realized only if they learn to manage their time, to develop strong study skills, and to handle stress, rather than be consumed by it. You, too, have a wealth of potential, and this booklet can help you discover that potential and learn how to invest it in your future. If you want to achieve what many only dream of, read on.

Ellen Kerwin –
An Early Beginning

Ellen grew up in a family that regularly discussed medicine. Three of her uncles are physicians– a pediatrician, an internist, and a cardiothoracic surgeon. Four of her older cousins are in residency programs throughout the United States, and one of them is Ellen's closest friend. "Sue and I talked a lot about becoming physicians," Ellen recalled. "We encouraged each other." Encouragement: That was how it started.

As Ellen grew up, she had many opportunities to learn more about medical practices. She worked part time for her uncle, the pediatrician. In addition to taking some patient histories, Ellen was able to watch him examine his young patients and perform some minor office surgical procedures. As his guest, she occasionally watched a team of physicians perform major surgery.

By the time Ellen started high school, she was certain about her career choice. "I wanted to be a pediatrician in a general practice, perhaps specializing in something like allergies," she remembered. Her determination was reflected in the way she approached her high school courses. Even then, she knew what she wanted.

Teachers recall how Ellen burrowed into biology, chemistry, and physics. "She always tried to relate what we studied to human medicine," one teacher commented. Though she found mathematics less interesting, she forced herself to study and to understand this material. Her cousins reminded her that trigonometry and calculus would help build a foundation crucial to success in college courses.

Her cousins also emphasized the importance of sound study habits. "You won't have much time in college or medical school," they told her. "What time you have must be used wisely and not squandered on distractions."

Ellen listened and worked hard to develop a routine that included time for study, participation in high school activities and some socializing with friends. She was also an excellent pianist and wanted to fit in time for practice and for playing alone, just to relax. Her parents helped Ellen set up a weekly schedule and pointed out what this organization enabled her to accomplish. Not only were Ellen's grades excellent, but she also gained confidence in her ability to succeed in several areas other than school. Ellen had become a doer, and she made time work for *her*.

Ellen attributes much of her success to motivation. "It was the reason for my daily routine. With a schedule, I concentrated on important activities. Every success in school moved me closer to becoming a physician," she emphasized. Ellen understood the importance of every step along her way. She didn't succeed by dreaming; she took control of her life by taking control of *time*.

Her high school years were pleasant, productive and generally free of worry. Only minor problems came up– an unexpected flat tire, a lost textbook or an argument with a friend– never anything considered really serious. "We had drugs in the school and alcohol at parties," she said. "I drank a little but just didn't like the taste, and drugs scared me."

With motivation, self confidence, family support, and a long list of successes, Ellen approached college with enthusiasm. She was able to handle the academic challenges quite well.

As a high school student and later in college, Ellen avoided a problem which many bright individuals face. Although tempted to race ahead to finish sometimes boring assignments, she concentrated on details, rechecked work, and prepared for all examinations. On occasions, she reviewed for examinations with groups of students; each group had special sections they discussed, making the meetings valuable.

In addition to seeing her academic accomplishments as steps toward medical school, Ellen derived a great deal of personal accomplishment from consistently doing well. With intelligent organization, she was able to use her talent. Discipline and planning brought out her abilities. She came to expect success but luckily never took it for granted.

That she was able to stay on a success track is impressive because of an unplanned major happening during her first semester in college, one that appeared very quickly and was completely unanticipated. She and a close friend from high school decided to room together. Shortly after classes began, her roommate began going with a junior in the same dormitory. They were inseparable.

"They were always in our room when I wanted to study or just relax," Ellen complained. "I tried to be patient and make polite suggestions. Nothing happened! I didn't have the energy at the time to fight and argue."

Ellen had to find out-of-the-way places to study but never was able to use her room, expecting her roommate and friend to be there when she arrived or come trooping in. Despite the stress of those weeks, Ellen vowed not to let up and didn't.

"I took cat naps in the student union or in the resident advisor's room. I wasn't ashamed to admit I was tired and needed sleep to function. She really helped me talk out my anger, so it didn't get in the way of studying. Some nights I slept on her floor or at a friends' room because going home was just impossible."

Studying and surviving her roommate's "thing" wore her out. "I went to class, studied, ate and tried to rest somewhere," she said. Ellen lost a friend, permanently, and 15 pounds. Finally, after Thanksgiving, she was able to move in with someone else and begin to lead a more normal life.

Unfortunately, many students do not have the determination and discipline Ellen demonstrated. She could call on her unflagging commitment to medicine which carried her through a most difficult time.

No matter how academically prepared you are, bumps and jams will appear. There could be an unanticipated problem like Ellen's or difficulty at home. Some difficulties can be overcome by applying common sense and sound judgement. Remember your instincts and rely on them to help you decide, and don't hesitate to ask others whose opinions you value. By realizing that some of these problems or difficulties have to be endured because you can't solve them, and by seeking help from professionals on your campus, you will be better able to cope and to continue on course toward your goal.

As you will see in Jane Delio's case, some pressures can be anticipated and handled by effective organization and a healthy attitude.

Jane Delio –
Determined Not To Slip

Not everyone is fortunate enough to start out like Ellen, with a family full of physicians to motivate and support them.

Jane began thinking of a career in nursing when she was hospitalized for an injury. As an athletic youngster, Jane enjoyed taking risks. When a rope on which she was swinging broke, she fell and fractured her right leg in two places. Not an auspicious beginning? Wrong!

The nurses who cared for Jane sparked her interest in this health care profession. She asked them how they knew so much and why they enjoyed working with sick people. "The sense of satisfaction that comes with helping people get well" was one comment Jane always remembered. "I'd like to do that," Jane thought. That was the dreamer in her speaking. But what about the doer?

From that moment on, Jane developed an interest that eventually became a goal. "My decision was actually made in the hospital when I was 10," Jane said. About that time, she also developed a passion for sports, particularly swimming and track. Jane enjoyed the challenge of improving her athletic abilities and besting opponents in competition.

In contrast to Ellen's family, neither of Jane's parents had graduated from high school. Both worked outside the home, and Jane, racing home after sports practice, had the extra responsibility of helping prepare dinner for her younger brother and sister. "We didn't talk much about careers, let alone my going into a nurse training program," Jane said.

Without guidance or much support from her parents or others in the family, Jane struggled in middle school and her first year in high school. Her grades were mediocre and she found paying attention in class increasingly difficult. Her dream of becoming a nurse was just that– a distant dream.

She mentioned her hope once or twice to her high school coaches who also taught biology and chemistry. "You can do better academically and still have time for sports," they each told her. They suggested she set aside three study periods of at least an hour every day: one each for science, mathematics, and English or foreign language. "Get up early to study so you are refreshed and the house is quiet," one coach told her. Jane used her one study period in school and the first hour after dinner to study, also helping her brother and sister with their homework.

One coach told Jane to concentrate on her subjects with the same single-minded intensity she used when swimming or running. Jane took his advice and found she not only understood her studies better, but she actually began to enjoy the learning process. As a result, Jane, the doer, who started poorly, had an above average scholastic record at the end of high school and finished in the middle of her high school class.

Because Jane was able to fit in sports and home duties, she felt confident about handling a nursing curriculum and a job to pay most of her tuition. Her parents grudgingly agreed to her decisions, allowing her to live at home without paying rent.

Ellen entered a major university at the same time Jane enrolled in a local community college. Both began to prepare for their careers with motivation and confidence in their ability to succeed. Their confidence was based in large measure on the knowledge that they could accomplish whatever they set their minds to because they could organize their lives effectively.

Because she had to work 20 to 30 hours each week, Jane was more determined than Ellen to use every minute carefully. "I liked the telephone answering jobs best because there was time to study," she said. Despite the pressure on her to earn money and help out at home, Jane never lost her determination. In fact, she appreciated the opportunity more because of her investment in it.

Unfortunately, John Chandler didn't start off as well. Not only was his motivation unclear, but John was poorly organized. When he tried to use the haphazard study habits that had worked in high school, he discovered that they were completely out of place in a demanding preprofessional curriculum. John became a success only when he learned the lessons that Ellen had known all along and that Jane discovered with the help of interested teachers. He was nearly too late!

John Chandler's Dangerous Approach

John Chandler's high school years were easy, too easy. "They were a breeze," he recalled. "Competition was light and teachers didn't expect too much. I was active in two clubs, served as a class officer, had a part-time job at a supermarket, and maintained an A- average."

With few exceptions, teachers in high school accepted his minimal performance and rarely challenged him to do better. John fell into the habit of waiting until the last minute to complete assignments or to study for examinations. Cramming was his style, as was studying all night before major examinations.

Like Ellen, John had relatives and close family friends in the health professions. He was particularly impressed by a cousin who ran a large pharmacy in a major hospital. Being able to combine medicine and management intrigued him. He considered pharmacy a career option but without the clear determination to "become" which Ellen and Jane had. "The connection between doing well in my courses in college and a career in pharmacy didn't really occur to me," John admitted. So, he merely got by.

High school teachers who felt John could do better gave him only general advice. "You could do much better," one science teacher advised. "You do your assignments well, but hastily. And you study too late to really absorb the material. You cram in facts for an exam and forget them soon afterward. Remember how much of the midterm exam material the class couldn't recall just one week later? That kind of studying will have to change if you want to succeed in college!"

Other teachers who had seen John's written work told him that last minute preparation would lead to problems as an undergraduate. An English teacher reminded John that college instructors wouldn't give him the benefit of the doubt when grading his papers. "You have good ideas but don't take the time to develop them. Competing for good grades at the university will probably demand that time," she warned.

A cousin reinforced what the science and English teachers had said: "University life is a different world. Everyone in required science and math

11

courses will be bright. Beginning with your very first semester, the competition will be tremendous. No more just getting by," he cautioned. John listened but didn't take his cousin very seriously. "He must be exaggerating," John thought. "Things can't be that tough! And after all, I did pretty well in high school without studying much." He spent his spare time in over extended bull sessions with friends, always with one better to tell.

"Just remember, no one will be around to remind you to study," his cousin continued. "And the campus is full of interesting and worthwhile distractions, not to mention all the time wasters. I was in a residence hall with a lot of smart kids who did poorly because they let time slip away."

"Better listen to your cousin." John's parents emphasized. "You have the ability to succeed. Give yourself the time! Don't waste energy on clubs or video games until you figure out how to make good grades!"

Five people who cared about John had offered well-meaning but general directions: They urged him to work harder, to try not to be distracted, to take more time to do a good job, and to prepare for an extremely competitive environment. The suggestion that he find more time for his studies registered, but he thought the answer was not to participate in clubs and to reduce his social life. John believed that without these distractions he would have plenty of time to study, but he was wrong.

Unfortunately, John had no plan to use the time available to him. He had learned on his own how to cram at the last moment and how to work feverishly under deadline pressure. He had never considered studying consistently– at the same time and in the same place– each day. It didn't occur to him to review regularly in order to integrate past and present assignments. As a result, John's study habits and overall time management hardly changed. He turned down invitations to join prehealth professions societies such as AED and other clubs, insisting, "Nothing is going to keep me from studying."

"Nothing" actually did interfere a great deal during his first two semesters. On a typical day, John spent his time as described in Illustration 1.

ILLUSTRATION 1. ONE DAY IN JOHN'S LIFE

9:30 a.m.	Awoke late after an evening of watching television and in bull sessions with friends; had to rush to get ready to attend a 9:50 class.
11:00 a.m.	Returned to the residence hall with intentions to study; actually watched a television game show until lunch.
12-1 p.m.	Ate lunch and played a few video games.

1-3 p.m.	Attended afternoon classes.
3-6 p.m.	Returned to residence halls for another attempt at study; actually listened to music and played a board game.
6-7 p.m.	Ate supper.
7-10 p.m.	Watched television and talked to friends in the residence hall lounge.
10-12 p.m.	Attempted to study, got bored, and fell asleep trying.

When John reviewed this day's activities, he reluctantly admitted that he spent little time actually studying. He also agreed that studying in the residence hall was difficult, if not impossible. "The noise was terrible," John said. "Guys wandered into my room to talk or invite me to play a video game. I couldn't concentrate on completing reading assignments or math problems."

"I planned to go to the library, but staying in the residence hall was just too easy," John recalled. "My books, notes, stereo, and board games were there." He also mentioned television sets in the residence hall lounge and friends' rooms as another reason for returning there after class. John became a fan of a few afternoon soap operas and part of an informal club that met to watch them almost every day. He could tell the story line of a few favorites backwards and forwards. Those "facts" he remembered.

John also spent odd hours between class on campus in the student union chatting, playing video games, or playing bridge. He barely found time for occasional concerts, speeches by visiting celebrities, and a few sporting events. Early in the semester, John was relaxed and confident. Thinking of the many weeks before the midterm exams, John persistently believed he had plenty of time and put off study for "later." John was shocked when he discovered that "later" didn't exist.

Although John had a course schedule and attended classes, he didn't know the exact dates of major examinations or when assignments were due. In early October, instructors in three courses reminded John and fellow students of those dates. When he suddenly realized that major deadlines were at hand, he panicked. John wasn't prepared because:

- His notes were poorly organized and contained some sections he couldn't understand.
- Sketchy outlines were all he had to begin two papers.
- The material to be emphasized on midterm examinations wasn't clear

to him, and he had also missed the review sessions that teaching assistants conducted in his chemistry, biology, and mathematics courses.

As a result, John prepared for midterm examinations and completed assignments under a great deal of pressure, knowing he wouldn't do well. In his anxiety, John jumbled formulas, dates, and basic concepts while cramming for tests. His instructors said his papers contained good ideas but were poorly written with many misspellings as well as badly edited. His papers were graded accordingly.

At midterm, John had a B-/C+ average. To make matters worse, he had received a C on the introductory chemistry midterm examination. In his anticipated major, John could hope for no more than a B. At the end of the first semester, John had a solid B- average. Although he raised one grade from C to B, his grade point average was just below the B level. But he couldn't raise his overall average at all in the spring.

SHAKEN CONFIDENCE

As the second semester progressed, John began to doubt his ability more and more. He grew more tense and disappointed as grades failed to improve and admission to a professional school seemed more unlikely. The harder he tried to work under assignment and examination deadline pressures, the poorer the result.

Unfortunately, John began to tell himself that he was going to fail. He was becoming convinced that he was destined to make poor grades, regardless of how much he tried to improve them. The relaxed and confident young man of September became a nervous and unhappy second-term freshman. He was full of doom and gloom– so different from Ellen and Jane.

While John struggled, Ellen and Jane were beginning academic careers that put them at or near the top of their class. They also found a little time to participate in campus organizations and to enjoy social and cultural activities at their schools. They got off to a successful start because they had realistically evaluated the difficult challenges of college life. They anticipated and overcame the problems experienced by poorly prepared freshmen. In particular, Ellen and Jane were aware of four potential problems too many freshmen face. John had to learn them the hard way before his successful turnaround began. What do you think those four problems are? Before you go on to the next section, jot down your ideas in the space below.

1. _____

2. _____

3. _____

4. _____

1. **A New Setting.** College or university life is often disconcertingly different from the easy going, pressure-free environments of many high schools. This is true regardless of the size of the college or university. A small liberal arts college may be no larger than a suburban or urban high school; it may even be smaller. An urban community college can be large and impersonal. But large or small, a college or university is an intensely competitive environment. Students at two-year colleges enrolled in health professions or transfer curriculums face similar challenges. Preprofessional and other students who must do well academically throughout their college careers find themselves under greater pressure than ever.

   To compound that problem, instructors often seem distant and unsupportive. But these aren't the only factors that make college life difficult. Students have a great deal of freedom and many worthwhile and marginal distractions to occupy their time. Every out-of-class hour of a student's day can be occupied by nonacademic activities. Freshmen used to the discipline of high school may be particularly entranced by all the "free time" and the variety of interesting ways to use it. Socializing, meeting friends, and just relaxing eats up hours. Time can slip by, and with it, opportunity.

2. **"Later On" and "Mental Panic."** "You can't separate the critical from the trivial at the last moment," a sophomore Ellen knew explained to her. "Real learning takes place as you have time to think about course material and fit the pieces together," her sophomore friend advised her. "You can't really learn at the last minute, although you may temporarily memorize material. You can't read for understanding." Imagine what happens to students trying to cram in everything at the last minute.

   Fatigue causes confusion and leads to poor performances on examinations. Written assignments or projects are not done well. With just a few days, or worse, a few hours left to complete term projects students panic when they can't review or prepare adequately. They undergo a form of mental paralysis that diminishes their ability to function. When this happens, their minds wander, and study or assignment preparation becomes virtually impossible.

Students who must work part-time or who are heavily involved in athletics *and do well* realize each hour is valuable. They plan how to use time before and after class, work, and practice. "Later on" is even more dangerous for them. They know when energy to study will be best and carefully guard those times.

Students who fail to plan each semester tend to adopt the "later on" approach Ellen and Jane were advised to avoid. "Later on" students don't plan their calendars, and, because of this, they quickly fritter away valuable hours. This is the third problem Ellen and Jane were determined to avoid.

3. **An Open Calendar.** Ellen's sophomore friend and many of her other friends always carried personal calendars. They had the habit of reviewing their calendars daily and weekly and planned daily schedules with carefully designated study times. These students used their calendars to support a routine that emphasized studying before other activities. "Later on" students were often surprised by rapidly approaching deadlines they'd somehow forgotten. Lacking a routine, these students were frequently distracted and wasted hours without knowing it. In John's case, inadequate preparation resulted from relying on a poor memory, rather than a good calendar. The calendar can prompt busy students to plan time to study, prepare for class, and work on assignments well before deadline pressure begins to build. It is a guide, a list of goals and objectives to be checked regularly, to be sure responsibilities are being handled and over commitment is avoided. For many students, this calendar substitutes for the guidance that parents and teachers once provided. Students without some form of reminder suffer a fourth problem– an absence of true learning time.

4. **"True Learning?–What Is It?"** John tried to study in a noisy residence hall full of distractions. He was an easy target for people who wandered through the dorms looking for someone to talk to or waste time with. As his schedule indicated, John set aside no time specifically for continuous study in one or more courses. He gave scant thought to finding a place where he could work without distractions. As a result, John had

little time to "get into" his studies. He either interrupted himself or allowed fellow students to drop in for a chat. John ended study sessions with a fuzzy sense of what he had read, few summarizing notes, and very low self-confidence. Because he often crammed under pressure, John had no time to think about a course or about its relationship to preparation for pharmacy school. Subjects John should have enjoyed, particularly in the sciences, became unusually difficult.

Consider how these four problems affected him each day. From the first, they began to put him under more and more destructive stress; let's call it *distress*. By October, he felt that no amount of study could improve his situation. He prepared assignments believing he couldn't make better grades. Every setback, such as a low quiz grade or a C on an assignment, made John feel he couldn't succeed. In a sense, John talked himself into failure. He was experiencing an aspect of distress which let him emphasize what he couldn't do. All of us experience some pressure: Parents can exert it, expecting consistently outstanding performance; roommates can disturb your study, relaxation, or sleep; boy and/or girl friends can make demands on both your time and energy; and social commitments add even another element. If the academic side isn't under control, imagine how difficult daily life can be.

A TURNAROUND

John's turnaround began when his motivation to build a career in pharmacy was rekindled. When John started to complain about what he couldn't do, his cousin kicked him in the pants. "Why are you giving up so soon?" he asked. "Pharmacy has a lot to offer."

After discussing those opportunities, his cousin challenged John to consider if he wanted a professional career. For much of the summer, John thought about pharmacy and his future.

By the beginning of his sophomore year, John Chandler had decided that he truly wanted to become a pharmacist. To do that, he had to raise a B-/C+ average to nearly a B+ level by the end of that academic year. "Why do I want to become a pharmacist?" John asked himself. He thought about what he might enjoy doing, the income possibilities, and the settings in which he would work. John then wrote down all the reasons why this career might be a strong possibility for him. After he reviewed the list, John wasn't positive about a career in pharmacy, but he was sure enough that he wanted to stay in the health professions to continue with the required courses. "Taking them gives me other alternatives in health or science careers," John decided. This is when his health professions advisors helped him by sharing insights about alternative health careers.

Have you considered your reasons for wanting a health professions career? Before you examine John's, list your own.

What Are Your Reasons? List Them Below.

1. _____

2. _____

3. _____

4. _____

5. _____

ILLUSTRATION 2. JOHN'S REASONS TO PURSUE A HEALTH PROFESSIONS CAREER

---

1. *Service and satisfaction.* This combination was the first reason John identified. When two members of his family were extremely ill, many individuals, in addition to physicians, had done a great deal to help heal his father and brother. John sensed their dedication and saw the satisfaction they derived from their work. John felt working in a hospital or clinic offered him an opportunity "to make a difference"; in fact, these were the words he used to describe the most significant motivation.

2. *Prestige.* John admitted that he would enjoy the respect and status this profession held. His cousin told him about the expanded role pharmacists are playing in health care delivery, beyond simply filling prescriptions. John really savored the idea of doing worthwhile work and being recognized for it at the same time.

3. *Challenge.* The many challenges the field offered ranked third on John's list of motivators. With new forms of treatment and medicines becoming available, hospital or clinic work would be "exciting" as he described it. Although acknowledging the routine, John mentioned the likelihood of unusual situations that would make each day different. Managing a department and making it

operate effectively was another engaging challenge. "I'll never be rich but more than likely have steady employment," he thought. "Hospitals and clinics will need pharmacists with business management ability. My lifestyle can be comfortable."

4. *Potential for change.* From pharmacy, John felt he could go into other areas of health-related business. Managing a clinic or some department in a hospital was a possibility. He began to realize that preprofessional courses and even entry in a course of study were a point of departure.Several directions were possible with a strong academic record.

With renewed motivation, John began to believe in himself and his ability to succeed. Instead of waiting to fail, John became determined to do well and took steps to organize his time and to study effectively. At this point, his approach was the same as Ellen's and Jane's. They were organized not only because of a strong desire to enter medicine and nursing but also to enjoy a successful college career. To them enjoyment meant doing well academically but not spending all their time in class or studying. The two goals were complementary and produced simple, effective plans to use time intelligently. Those plans enabled them to:

- Plan an entire semester and set aside regular study periods.
- Find a place where they could study for two or three hours at a time.
- Organize material for each course so they could review and complete current assignments.
- Find time to relax with friends, and in Ellen's case, to participate in a few campus organizations.
- Manage, as did Jane, the dual responsibility of going to school while working at a part-time job.

In fact, they established goals for each day that contributed in some way to their career goal of becoming health professionals. Ellen and Jane used small successes to keep up their motivation. "I'm on the way," they told themselves when completing a course assignment or doing well on a quiz. Those regular successes kept their enthusiasm high because each one was a step toward their major goal.

All the students who were interviewed in preparation of this booklet agreed that long-term and short-term goals motivated them to organize. They also were in control because they understood the meaning of self-discipline.

Ellen and Jane enrolled as freshmen with six goals carefully defined, and they kept a list of those goals on their desks as a continuing reminder. They wanted to:

- Gain acceptance into the professional school of their choice.

- Thoroughly understand material presented in required preprofessional courses.

- Have the time to truly enjoy learning rather than be forced to frantically cram in facts and formulas.

- Prepare in advance by using their extra time to read and do other assignments for the pleasure of it.

- Grow and mature by getting to know students from different backgrounds and by participating in organized campus activities.

- Be aware of the educational resources available to them and know how to use these resources.

Both young women had help seeing the relationship between achieving goals and realistic time management: Ellen's family provided her with role models and guidance; and Jane's teachers and coaches showed her how to transfer athletic motivation to academic pursuits.

Unfortunately, as many academic advisors report, John, like many other students, began college with no clear motivation and little self-discipline. Devastated by initial setbacks, some of them change majors or leave school. A few are lucky and like John learn in college how to achieve success like Ellen's and Jane's. The John Chandler's start their comebacks by taking a long, hard look at their goals and by realizing how much achieving those goals means to them; then their determination to succeed is revitalized.

John's reasons for a pharmacy career motivated him in two distinct ways. He worked harder in all his courses to gain admission to pharmacy school. By acquiring a strong business background, other career options opened up for him. He then began thinking about what he had to do each day to develop an excellent academic record and to prepare for admissions examinations. At this point, his method of preparing for examinations, organizing, and managing time began to resemble Ellen's and Jane's. All three of them:

1. Identified each semester's academic goals– not grades alone, but an understanding of materials covered in major subjects that would build a foundation for success in a professional school.

2. Established limits on what they could accomplish, giving priority to

major activities such as review and assignment preparation to achieve the academic goals they listed.

3. Prepared a semester plan enabling them to organize an appropriate amount of study and preparation time, as well as fit in other responsibilities such as Jane's jobs.

4. Set aside time for limited involvement in organizations and other campus activities for relaxation, athletics, and fun with friends.

5. Developed a method to master material and prepare assignments and found locations where they could concentrate.

To reinforce these elements, they used different techniques. These techniques became habits and led to routines that produced control over busy days and led to academic excellence. For all three, *identifying goals* and *setting limits* were the important first steps in their plans.

Even with the best-laid plans, detours occur, as Ellen discovered with her roommate problem. But the problems will likely be fewer, and you will be better prepared to handle them. You will spend less time and energy worrying about the "what if's" because you know coping with pressure is part of life. Past successes strengthen your confidence.

Goals and Limits

Ellen, Jane, and John planned each semester, establishing a routine to be followed by the end of the first week of classes. They set aside study periods after lectures, laboratory, and discussion sections had been identified.

Jane was very careful to arrange her study sessions around her part-time jobs. She was careful to allow enough time to get to work and back to campus. She looked for jobs that offered opportunities to study at work and where flexible hours could be arranged.

In addition to a routine, Ellen, Jane, and John considered their course load and the amount of time required to do well in all classes. Before each semester began, they talked to former students of the courses they currently were taking about the effort required and particular problems they might expect. After considering factors such as competition, the difficulty of material, examinations, and assignments, they allocated appropriate study time according to these factors. On occasion, they even dropped a course because they realized the load would have been too heavy.

With that plan, they had sufficient time to master material, to systematically prepare for examinations, and to complete assignments for each course. During their second year, all three began to schedule time for review of material likely to appear on entrance examinations for professional school.

Illustration 3 is a weekly calendar used one semester. As the illustration indicates, they also found time for activities, relaxation, and sports. They were not studying nor attending class 100 percent of the day. All three were adamant about the importance of "balance" achieved by getting away from books and class notes. They felt better and generally returned refreshed to studies after a swim, club meeting or dinner with friends. Most importantly, they followed a routine, making changes only when absolutely necessary.

Of the three, Jane had to do the most careful day-to-day planning because of work and continuing family responsibilities. Hers was a balancing act to make sure she met her financial needs as well as prepared adequately for class. Jane also realized that balance wasn't always possible. Hours on the job had to be cut down to prepare for an examination or to complete a project. On some days, after a late night at work, she came less prepared to class.

Each of them spent a few minutes each Sunday afternoon thinking about the week. They wrote down upcoming events that required special attention, including nonacademic activities such as laundry, meetings, and social events and clipped that list to their personal calendars. Fewer surprises and lower tension levels were the results of this planning activity.

The three experienced less panic because they'd written down important tasks and critical details, rather than trusting fragile memories. Not only did they carry personal calendars, they had another copy to keep on their desks, giving them two reminders to follow their routines. They also used the plan to minimize "task creep" or the tendency to take on more activities while forgetting what had to be done. Jane even used a calendar program along with a basic word processing package and was able to identify major deadlines and examination dates.

John, in particular, used his calendar to remind him of priorities before agreeing to a social event or additional involvement in a club; as a result, saying no became easier.

Ellen, Jane, and John were computer literate and used their own college equipment. They edited their research papers many times, stored and retrieved their notes, and searched library data sources for the necessary information.

ILLUSTRATION 3. A TYPICAL WEEKLY CALENDAR

Weekly Study Schedule

	MON.	TUES.	WED.	THURS.	FRI.	SAT.	SUN.
7 - 8	Dress Breakfast	Dress Breakfast	Dress Breakfast	Dress Breakfast	Dress Breakfast	Sleeping	
8 - 9	CHEMISTRY	ENGLISH	CHEMISTRY	ENGLISH	CHEMISTRY	Clean room	
9 - 10	Review Psych	Speech	Review Psych	Practice	Review Psych	Shopping	Sleep
10 - 11	PSYCHOLOGY	Speech	PSYCH	Speech	PSYCH	etc.	Church
11 - 12	Review History	SPEECH	Review History	SPEECH	Review History		
12 - 1				LUNCH			
1 - 2	HISTORY	open	HISTORY	open	HISTORY	Library	Recreation
2 - 3	CHEM LAB	PHYS ED	Compose	PHYS ED	Chem	Work on	and/or
3 - 4		Chem	Speech	Psych	Chem	papers	reading and
4 - 5		Chem		Psych	Recreation & Laundry	Recreation	work on
5 - 6	Lab Report	open	open	open			papers
6 - 7				DINNER			
7 - 8	English	Psych	Finish English	Chem	Recreation	Recreation	Psych
8 - 9	English	Psych	Theme	Chem			Psych
9 - 10	History	Start English	more work on	History			History
10 - 11	History	Theme	Speech	History			History

There is No Substitute for Daily Preparation

THREE-RING MONITORING AND TASKCREEP

These successful students developed a three-ring monitoring approach designed to minimize task creep– an approach they will use probably throughout their professional careers. The three rings are shown in Illustration 4. The inner ring, the most important one, is labeled *must*. By preparing a weekly schedule, all three students identified their major responsibilities and entered them in this ring.

1. Class attendance

2. Study periods

3. Work

4. Limited participation in clubs or organizations

5. Time for relaxation

By reviewing their planning calendars regularly, Ellen, Jane, and John were likely to restrict rather than expand activities. In fact, their ability to say no to activities outside the inner must ring grew stronger every semester.

When activities or opportunities outside the five in the must ring appeared, they paused to evaluate before responding. That is where the other two rings helped. The second *maybe* ring was for involvements that could be considered, not necessarily accepted, and included the following:

• Attempting an additional course project.

• Reading beyond what was assigned.

• Holding office in a campus organization.

• Chairing or being in a major leadership position for a campus social or charitable event.

ILLUSTRATION 4. THREE RING ACTIVITY MONITORING

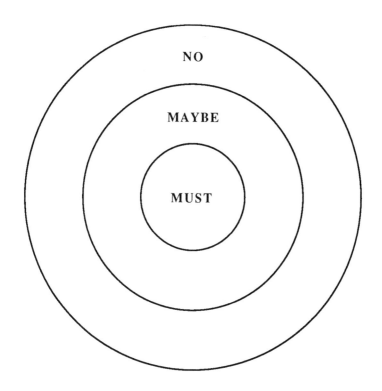

"Maybe" activities are often more time-consuming than they appear. Left unchecked, they can overpower the inner ring.

During the pause to evaluate, these students decided whether they could handle another responsibility. On some occasions, they said yes, as for example:

- John was an officer in Alpha Epsilon Delta his junior and senior year but he turned down the offer to become president because he knew how much time it would take.
- Ellen was a volunteer tutor working with high school students experiencing problems learning mathematics, but she never spent more than four hours per week tutoring.
- Jane was on the committee planning social events at the community college. She was especially careful to take on only limited tasks which would fit with her other duties, especially her part-time jobs.

As a rule, these students were more likely to say no than to take on additional responsibilities. They agreed to chair committees or participate in extra class projects only when they knew these activities wouldn't take time away from their studies. They also wanted to protect valuable relaxation and fun time. All three wanted a liveable pace, not an exhausting one.

All three learned to stay away from the outer "no" or "never" ring. This ring contains the dangerous time-sapping activities that seemed so nonthreatening to John during his first difficult semester: the apparently innocent video games, the "occasional" bridge matches, the friendly meetings of soap opera buffs.

All three learned to stay away from activities in this ring unless they knew they were well-prepared for classes. And when they relaxed, they didn't worry about coursework. As a result, they enjoyed parties, intramural sports, concerts, or evenings with friends more completely. These students knew what was important. Do you?

What are your inner- and outer-ring activities? In the space below, identify the few activities that should be a central concern this semester. Then shift attention to the outer ring and decide what distraction and time wasters you should avoid. You may want to keep these lists available as a reminder during the semester. Consider posting the lists you are about to make near your desk or in some other prominent location.

For This Semester, My Inner-Ring Activities Are:

1. _____

2. _____

3. _____

4. _____

5. _____

The "No" Ring Activities to Avoid Include:

1. _____

2. _____

By emphasizing the inner "must" ring, you automatically make studying the highest priority. As those regular periods become habits, you'll have a better chance to concentrate on your coursework. The three students found themselves getting excited about learning. Each reported a new ability to grasp basic concepts and then to put facts into a context so that these facts could be remembered as part of the whole and recalled on examinations more easily.

With this study routine and concentration, all three found that preparation for major examinations proceeded more smoothly. They were able to integrate that preparation with other responsibilities. They enjoyed their studies, and for John, this was a most surprising and rewarding development. That enjoyment came from concentration and the excitement it produced.

CONCENTRATION AND SUSTAINED INTENSITY

Remember how easily John Chandler was distracted as he attempted to study in the residence hall? Noise and constant interruptions made concentrating difficult, if not impossible, for him. His mind regularly drifted to work he hadn't completed. This is an especially dangerous trap for highly intelligent students. Their attention will skip ahead to consider other options or questions the material may raise. The brightest students are often the ones who must remind themselves most frequently that they must concentrate on one task at a time.

In addition, he was constantly tempted to stop studying. Friends came in to chat and invited him to join discussions, to play bridge, or to watch a favorite television program. Because John wasn't determined to study, he willlingly accepted those invitations.

Initially, John wasted time on an assortment of distractions that took precedence over his studies. "After all, there will always be time later in the day or tomorrow," he rationalized. In reality, John hadn't changed his approach to studying, he still subconsciously relied on last-minute preparation for examinations or assignments. But John had too much to do, and he didn't understand some material. As a high school student, John was able to study or finish assignments just before a test or deadline. He felt a little pressure, but he was in control of the situation. Conditions changed dramatically in college; with too much to remember or to do, he panicked.

After his turnaround, John was able to use blocks of time effectively to read, review notes, solve problems, or prepare assignments. Ellen, Jane, and John discovered the five following major benefits as a result of their regular high-concentration study periods:

1. They wanted to start studying at the same time and in the same place every day. They had a sense of being *pulled* there in such a way that invitations to distractions were easily refused. They identified specific assignments to be completed at a study session and looked forward to accomplishing a narrow goal.

2. Their ability to focus on one task grew stronger, and they didn't waste valuable study hours daydreaming or needlessly worrying over remaining work. All three did more because of this undivided attention– and made fewer errors in computation or problem analysis, for example. They got "involved" or "into" the assignments as they were concentrating. The more they studied, wrote, or analyzed, the greater their understanding and excitement became. With increased confidence, they left each study session feeling a great sense of accomplishment. Concentration increased their ability to think about written assignments and to prepare them well. Outlines and several drafts using word processing programs also helped them enormously.

3. They didn't wander from task to task or self-interrupt. They stayed seated longer in a suitable location, gathering the necessary materials for completing an assignment before sitting down to work. If they reached a difficult point, they were more willing to work through it than to stop or to find something easier to do. Each established short-term study goals and used a limited amount of time to reach them. Jane knew exactly what she could study before and after going to work.

4. They were better able to get back on track after an interruption. If a friend requested help or if a telephone rang, they only stopped studying

temporarily. Because they were concentrating before the interruption, it was easier to remember the stopping point. They also recalled how much had been accomplished before the interruption and were enthusiastic about getting back to work. "Got to get back to work," or "Can we talk later?" were the phrases they used to end a visit or to diplomatically close a conversation.

5. The willingness to postpone certain distractions increased. Friends who invited them to take a break were often told politely, "Not now." They blocked out discussion in progress or tempting television programs. And when they really wanted to concentrate, they found out-of-the-way study places far from tempting distractions– disappearing for hours, emerging tired but satisfied. Friends couldn't find them to offer opportunities for procrastination. All campuses have such places: empty classrooms, sections of the library, or unused areas in residence halls.

Neither Ellen, Jane, nor John were taught how to concentrate by teachers or parents. Ellen and Jane were encouraged more than John to give certain activities great attention. "Think about one thing at a time," music instructors and athletic coaches repeated. From other experiences, Ellen and Jane had learned the value of focusing attention on one activity at a time. Swimming taught Jane the same valuable lesson piano practice taught Ellen: mastery of skills demanded steady concentration and brought an exciting sense of self-satisfaction. Knowing the value of concentration, they set aside specific blocks of time to spend in carefully chosen locations, thus focusing maximum attention on mastering coursework. After his difficult freshman year, John realized this, too.

You can experience similar success and learn how to concentrate so that you'll attain academic excellence. You can share Jane's, John's, and Ellen's success if you develop a routine that integrates time, study space, assignments, and a "locking in" process. With each accomplishment, your confidence will grow and course material will become stimulating and challenging. As a natural outcome of learning to concentrate, these students and others earned excellent grades, and so can you.

The next step is to experiment and develop your own routine. A final step involves selecting ways you can make concentration a regular activity each day.

1. Recall for a moment situations in which you gave one activity a great deal of attention. Consider competing in sports, playing a musical in-

strument, or reading an exciting novel. How did you feel? What were you able to do? Research on concentration has proven that when an individual focuses on a single task or assignment the following experiences usually occur:

- One activity receives full attention; what was done before or might be coming next isn't important.
- The environment can be blocked out so noise and other distractions are neither heard nor felt.
- The individual is self-confident and positive about doing well and tells him- or herself that.
- A mental picture of a successful outcome may appear in the mind's eye, heightening determination and self-confidence.
- Separation from the environment takes place, and the individual blends into the task, increasing the intensity and euphoria associated with its accomplishment.
- A "flow" or attachment develops between the individual and the activity, one so strong that stopping is difficult.

Experience these positive results by experimenting with the steps suggested next.

2. Learn to experiment. Determine and then remember when and where your attention is greatest. You know what can be accomplished if you start studying with both confidence and enthusiasm. Then determine when, where, and what you will concentrate on. To do this you must:

- Identify one or two periods during the day already set aside for study when your energy level will be high.
- Pick a location relatively free of distraction.
- Select portions of a major assignment you enjoy but find a bit difficult.
- Review the concentration development routine found in Illustration 5.
- Use the routine as the starting point for your own unique way to lock in and study with great enthusiasm and determination. Experimentation with the best time, place, and involving process will lead to a very personal method and eventually will evolve the self-disciplining routine mentioned earlier. As you succeed, your desire to concentrate will increase, and you'll apply your concentration skills to more subjects.

3. Learn to target your concentration on certain assignments or portions of assignments to give them this high level of attention. You'll learn to identify what should be studied when and where. As a study session begins, jot down your goals and use the list as a guide and a challenge. As you'll notice, rewards follow periods of intensive attention. These students find time to relax, to join organizations, and to enjoy the range of activities found on a college campus. They know how to apply concentration to reach narrow, achievable goals in a single study period.

John, Ellen, and Jane were highly motivated, determined to master material, and aware that time was a resource to use intelligently. Used intelligently, periods for concentration were set aside and protected. Each of them constructed a unique time management program composed of a few simple techniques that supported his or her efforts to achieve certain goals and master course material through concentration. After one or two semesters, all three students didn't have to think about managing time, but organized automatically.

To assist you in developing a personalized and effective approach to managing time, Ellen's, Jane's, and John's unique ways of managing time are described in the next section.

ILLUSTRATION 5. A FIVE-STEP PROCESS FOR "LOCKING IN"

Selection of task, time, and place enhances concentration. Once this is done, you are ready for the five-step process that leads to "locking in" on one task regardless of its appeal.

1. Define a goal. That goal reminds you of what must be done. With it, you can focus attention on one task at a time more easily. You even tell yourself to get going. By doing so, you reduce your tendencies to procrastinate. Imagine the pleasure of having unpleasant work completed and of being able to relax afterward.

2. Relax for a moment. A moment of relaxation helps you shut out the environment. Research shows that this step prevents the mind from wandering back to the work you've just finished or to the work you're about to begin.

3. Develop a mental picture. Imagine yourself actually doing the task. This enables you to see possible problems and helps you to

"visualize" the final product. This step helps focus concentration on the single task.

4. Take a few deep breaths. This fourth step begins the process that researchers call "locking in." Before a competitive event, athletes "lock in" and focus completely on their immediate goal.

5. Establish "flow" with a directing message. Flow, as used here, describes what happens when task and person blend together. Momentum is established. Talking to oneself establishes flow. You could say, for example: "I'm going to finish this theme at this study session," or "Before the next class, I'll summarize these lecture notes."

Challenge yourself to accomplish and visualize an excellent outcome.

Three Distinctive Styles

You needn't be a genius to complete a successful preprofessional program. You needn't have superhuman endurance. You needn't follow a rigorous program of self-denial. Just look at Ellen, Jane, and John. They're probably much like you. They're bright, young, and fun-loving. And they have distinct career goals. So why did they succeed where others have failed? For three reasons:

1. They believed in themselves.
2. They knew what they wanted.
3. They followed a simple, sensible self-management system.

As you review their systems, remember that you will be developing your *own* system, one that is best suited to your personality and environment. Choose the techniques that work for *you*, practice them with confidence, and always remember that every success you achieve is a step along the way to *your* goal. In Appendix 1, you will find a list of study techniques to consider, in addition to the ones these students used.

JOHN CHANDLER'S SYSTEM

John Chandler struggled to develop study habits that would let him master course material, but he learned to make time work for him. To begin with, he set aside *two 2 to 3 hour blocks of time each day* for study. Because of meetings or review sessions that he had to attend, John didn't study at the same time every day. But he never wavered from the two-session-per-day minimum and sometimes added a third. "I knew if I didn't study according to schedule, I'd pay for it with grade points," John explained.

As each session began, he prepared a plan similar to the one in Illustration 6. He used the blocks of time to concentrate and to make decisions about which material was important. With this organization, he was able to identify certain concepts as central and committed himself to mastering them at one session. He kept a supply of large note cards to write down major concepts, formulas, equations, and terms. The cards were especially helpful when reviewing alone or with groups.

Because John had guaranteed himself study time, he felt comfortable about limited participation in Trekkers, a campus hiking club. "I was happier after my freshman year because I'd joined this club," John said. "My main circle of friends was transformed– now they were people other than those I was competing with."

John pointed out that he stopped thinking constantly about his courses now that his life had more balance. With organization he was under less pressure. After meeting major study responsibilities, club activities became a reward.

ILLUSTRATION 6. PLAN FOR ONE 3 HOUR STUDY SESSION

---

1. Review notes from the last two physics lectures, underline key points, prepare summary on note cards.
2. Read Chapters 4-5 in physics text, sketch answers to end of chapter questions.
3. Outline English theme due in three weeks and write just the introduction.
4. Finish last five math problems.

Index Card Reminders

As a regular reminder, John developed an index card system. He would write down what had to be done each day on one card– this was his inner "must" ring. On another card he listed a "maybe" group that could wait a day: laundry and shopping, for example. Each day John tried to complete all the items on his must list, plus a few on the maybe one. At the end of each week, he could look back on a number of accomplishments on both lists. The cards become his memory for details, taking away the pressure associated with trying to remember one or two lonesome details. Every morning, he took a few minutes to prepare both cards.

Interruption Control

As John became more successful academically, he felt comfortable about participating in campus organizations. He spent more time making telephone calls and contacts with students on campus. When he became an officer in Alpha Epsilon Delta, the number of calls increased significantly. While some business was transacted, socializing consumed much time.

The 2 to 3 hours John set aside for study became fragmented by telephone calls. John controlled these interruptions by finding a quiet spot in the graduate library where he could study alone. John used a telephone answering machine to screen calls; he answered the most important ones and did other fraternity work after returning from studying. "I concentrated on my studies and limited myself to one social activity," John emphasized.

Worry Reduction

John began reviewing progress he had made with improved organization. "I understood the material and its importance," John recalled. "The basic concepts were clearer to me. Courses were more interesting, and my grades improved substantially."

By monitoring his progress, John began to worry less and spent study time reviewing notes, reading, or completing assignments. He didn't fret over what might happen. His motivation replaced anxiety, and his organization bolstered confidence.

"It is my system," John said somewhat proudly. "I don't want or need to spend every moment with my studies. Time away from the books with other students is refreshing and absolutely necessary." John's system isn't a complex one, nor should it be. After all, managing time is the means, not the end.

In addition to studying and to excelling, John was thinking and evaluating his initial career choice. He talked to advisors, to practicing pharmacists, and to hospital administrators. They suggested John consider a doctorate in pharmacy to increase his knowledge of drugs and potential employability. He also began to relate what he was learning in all courses to a possible career choice.

Basically, John has:

- Established a minimum of two blocks of time for study each day.
- Prepared note cards for each course to record key information for review purposes.
- Identified the important material to be addressed in each study block and avoided the trivial.
- Prepared note cards for each course to record key information for review purposes.
- Identified the important material to be addressed in each study block and avoided the trivial.

- Reminded himself each day with his index cards of tasks to be done.

- Handled fraternity responsibilities after academic responsibilities.

- Reduced worrying by emphasizing accomplishments.

- Evaluated possible career choices by talking to practicing professionals and his academic advisor and/or health advisor.

ELLEN KERWIN'S SYSTEM

Ellen Kerwin's system is somewhat different. She began to develop it in high school, with an emphasis on planning for an entire semester. As each semester began, she thought through how time would be allocated. In addition to a study schedule and time for a few other activities, Ellen noted important semester deadlines. Ellen had a monthly calendar similar to the one in Illustration 7 and could see at a glance what assignments were due and what examinations were approaching.

Ellen also thought about all the courses for a semester and how they were related in content. This thought prompted a unique method for studying that increased her interest in subjects and her ability to do well in them. With this system, she was motivated to use shorter periods of time available between classes to organize course material.

ILLUSTRATION 7. ELLEN'S MONTHLY CALENDAR

October 1987

Sunday	Monday	Tuesday	Wednesday	Thursday	Friday	Saturday
	1 Begin Studying for 10/8 Physics Test	2	3	4	5	6
7	8 Physics Test	9	10 Begin Work on Chemistry Problems	11	12 Chemistry Quiz	13
14	15	16	17 Start Outline for Psych Paper	18	19 Chemistry Problems Due	20 Prepare Discussion for English Class
21	22	23	24	25 Lead Discussion in English	26 Chemistry Quiz	27
28	29	30 Psych Outline Due	31			

Review– Summarization– Problem Identification

In the hours between classes or shortly afterward, Ellen immediately reviewed and summarized class notes. She rarely waited longer than a day to do this. "I was able to capture the essence of each lecture, highlight important concepts, and identify questions as they came up," Ellen said. "I reviewed material each day before beginning a new assignment. Sometimes I listened to tapes of lectures made to back up my notes. Hearing the lecture again helped me understand and remember."

If Ellen didn't understand a point in lecture notes she usually asked the instructor. "I can't remember ever not being able to obtain assistance," she recalled. "Every professor I approached was willing to help clarify a concept and take the time necessary to do it."

Ellen highlighted major concepts or facts in notes or textbooks and found this form of summary helpful when reviewing for an examination. Actually her practice of reviewing before examining new material made cramming unnecessary. "Last minute studying wasn't for me," Ellen emphasized. "I needed a good night's sleep before an examination."

Calm and Confident

On occasion, Ellen worked with a study group to review for an examination. Listening to others explain material or explaining it herself helped solidify the facts. "Attending review sessions graduate assistants conducted also clarified and reinforced key points," she said.

Ellen arrived about an hour before an examination for a final review and time to think about the material one more time. "It was almost a casual leafing through my notes," Ellen said. "I wasn't trying to absorb facts. My goal was to get into a calm mood so I could recall material more easily." She could only do this because of steady preparation and little or no last minute cramming.

Related Courses

When possible, Ellen tried to take courses that explored complementary subjects; she selected chemistry, biology, zoology, and genetics courses for their similarity. This made preparation easier because the material blended together. Ellen believed she could see the relationship of the concepts to preparation for medical school. "It made studying all the more exciting– seeing how these basics apply to human medicine."

Note File For Each Course

She kept together all the notes, diagrams, assignments, and miscellaneous items for each course. "I kept them in one place and lost little time looking for necessary material," she pointed out. After each lecture or laboratory session, she dated and filed each summary. As the semesters progressed, she developed a complete course file, which she regularly studied in preparation for the MCAT. Ellen did lighten her course load the semester of the MCAT to gain more time for preparation. With that organization and an excellent review course, Ellen did extremely well on this important examination.

"Me" Time

Every day, she took time just to relax. Little things were important, such as reading a novel, meeting friends for dinner, going to a movie or watching favorite television programs. "They come after or as a break," Ellen emphasized. "They are more than rewards, really necessities."

Daily Control

Ellen's system provided her with a sense of daily control. Her intense dislike of pressure was a primary motivation for her unique system. She also knew that these few techniques gave her an opportunity to participate in organizations, to spend time with friends, and to exercise daily. She knew she couldn't enjoy any of them if she didn't organize and accomplish her academic responsibilities. Ellen commented that the following techniques had become habits she will probably maintain in some form for the rest of her life, for as a physician, she will have notes to organize, journals to study, and a demanding schedule to maintain:

- She developed a semester plan that plotted all course activities, especially assignments and examinations.
- She established a relationship among courses that would tie together concepts and the facts related to them.
- She asked questions in class focused on interrelationships and to make sure she understood.
- She summarized notes from lectures or laboratories shortly after each session, identified problems or questions, and obtained answers from instructors.
- She reviewed at the same time she studied new material, sometimes doing this in hours between classes.
- She established a note file for each course so that all related material was in the same place.

- She set aside two or three times each week for routine duties. Whatever errands, laundry, or letters didn't get done had to wait until later, usually with no problem.
- She set aside "me time" every day.

JANE DELIO'S SYSTEM

Jane had to remind herself everyday of her goals: The major one was to become a nurse. This was a profession she felt would provide fulfillment and happiness, both important to her. Because of that belief, her first self-disciplining technique emerged in high school. Jane began to say no to a number of invitations she knew would consume hours needed for study. Having many friends with no career interests, she had to be careful of spending too much time with them. Family responsibilities meant she had to be extra careful about overextending herself.

Sense of Responsibilities

To avoid distractions, Jane wrote down major responsibilities, first on note cards and then on a calendar. At the start of each semester, she listed all courses and activities in which she planned to participate. Illustration 8 is a sample from the second semester of her second year. Jane had two such lists, one on her desk and another attached to her daily calendar. "Before taking on anything else, I naturally looked at this list," Jane reported. "Most of the time, these responsibilities led me to refuse another activity."

ILLUSTRATION 8. JANE'S LIMITED LIST

High Priority Must
Course Emphasis
Biology
Calculus
Chemistry
Dangers
Biology midterm
Calculus problems
Chemistry final
Other Activities
Swimming
Nursing Society Committee
Union Committee

One Study Location

Jane needed motivation to get away from the commotion at home. "There were too many people around and so much television noise," Jane explained. "I had to remind myself of what could be done in two or three hours at the college library." Like John, she found a quiet spot that became her principal study location. Jane found she was relaxed and able to focus on assignments in that location, away from friends and other distractions. After work, she could study at home in the kitchen, particularly rechecking notes and making up study guides. She also knew which subjects she could work on at her job, in spare moments between customers or answering the phone.

Goals For Each Study Session

When Jane sat down, she began by deciding about a goal for each study session. "I wanted to leave with a feeling of accomplishment," Jane reported. Because she had a part-time job, making best use of time was especially important. At the start, these goals were unrealistically ambitious: She attempted to read and summarize too many pages or to solve several complex problems in a short time. Jane learned to scale down expectations so she could achieve realistic goals. Illustration 9 is a list of what she planned and actually accomplished in one 3-hour period. Being naturally competitive, Jane found these goals a challenge and worked hard to reach them.

ILLUSTRATION 9. JANE'S STUDY SESSION PLAN

---

1. Finish algebra problems due in one week– set aside for review at next study session.
2. Organize chemistry notes for upcoming midterm examination– identify major areas to study.
3. Review outline for presentation to be given in speech class.

A Commitment To Learn

"It would have been easy to get into the memorize rut before examinations," Jane admitted. "Then I would cram and any appreciation of the course would have disappeared." As a result, Jane made a commitment to learn material and used three reminder questions to keep her on track.

1. How does this subject fit into my preparation for a career in nursing?

2. How can this material be related to other subjects I'm taking?
3. What is the best way to understand both the basic concepts and related facts?

Her commitment to master her material permanently rather than temporarily was a result of answering these three questions.

Time For Balance

Jane enjoyed a good time and also knew that breaks from study and her job were necessary. She made a decision after her first semester to join one club and to take on an activity she could handle. The two activities chosen met three criteria:

- She could learn something from the experience.
- They would be fun.
- She could meet new people at the college.

Jane chose to become a member of the student government social committee and of a group that tutored high school students with low grades. Jane helped one young woman from a family situation much like her own twice a week. She also swam regularly to relax and to keep reasonably fit.

These five techniques helped Jane stay on track and avoid distractions she knew could be dangerous. With family responsibilities and a 20-hour per week part-time job, staying organized to study and to prepare for all classes was essential. Jane lightened her course load because she knew that working was essential, as was doing well in every subject. "Better to handle less effectively than collapse with an overload," she believed.

- A sense of responsibilities led Jane to identify what was important each semester and to say no to other involvements.
- One study location became the place to which she returned each day.
- Goals for each study session increased her motivation because she established reachable targets.
- A commitment to learning reduced tendencies to cram and to temporarily memorize.
- Time for balance and participation was included in her calendar.

Though each student approached each day differently, they were all guided by an unwavering determination to control their own lives, rather than permit distractions to draw them away from their goals. This crucial factor compelled them to establish and follow daily routines.

Being organized was beneficial in other ways. Ellen, Jane, and John were able to anticipate problems and got help when necessary. All three attended review sessions for certain courses. Ellen asked instructors to clarify points which were not clear to her. Jane's advisor helped her with scheduling problems and gave her tips on how to do well in two major required courses.

They all found more experienced students, counselors, and advisors ready and able to listen. Instead of letting problems remain to worry and to frustrate, each of them sought advice. Sometimes it was to live through a difficult period. Other times, they were advised to take action, like quitting a job, dropping a course, or approaching an assignment differently. All three agree that seeking assistance is a clear sign of strength.

Jane and John, especially, grew more confident because of improved organization. Jane realized she could become a nurse, in spite of family and work demands. In addition to her own routine, Jane knew where to look for help at the community college.

John realized he was in a position to go in several career directions. He thought about pharmacy's advantages and disadvantages, talked with those in the field, and discussed options with his advisor.

Preparation for exams was steady, not last minute for all three of them. Review courses were just that, not first time learning. Ellen found her MCAT review course helped her underline key material and learn how to deal with complicated test questions.

Overall, they took advantage of stress' positive features and avoided many of its dangerously negative aspects, such as depression and sleepless nights.

CONCENTRATION AND DISTRESS MANAGEMENT

From the moment of birth, all of us are subject to stress. Among the many definitions of this phenomenon is "the response of a creature to his or her environment." As the late Hans Selye, a pioneer researcher in this area demonstrated, one stage of stress is positive and useful. *Eustress* is a condition in which one self-motivates and becomes intense about accomplishing a goal.

Other researchers, particularly Mihaly Czikszentmihali, a University of Chicago psychologist, maintain that "flow," an attachment between the individual and the task, is established. Performance levels increase because of the attachment and the self-confidence it produces. The more one becomes involved, the greater the happiness or euphoria.

And, interestingly, while there is intensity, individuals have an inner calm borne of self-confidence. In fact, those in a state of flow tell themselves work will be done well. Concentration is likely at this stage of stress. Flow makes it all the more possible. A clear sense of what must be done combined with self-confidence builds a level of controlled intensity.

John, Ellen, and Jane were able to concentrate because they became enthusiastic about thoroughly learning course material and carefully preparing assignments. A specific time and place for study became habit. They were mentally prepared to make effective use of a period of time each day.

Study session plans enabled them to focus on priorities. A routine similar to the one in the previous section started the concentration process. Discipline grew.

The stress phenomenon is diagrammed in Illustration 10. Researchers such as Selye and Gordon Van Amberg have isolated six stages. The first stage, *eustress*, is available to these three students regularly. As one result, they remain low on the distress line. When difficulties move them to the discomfort level, they take action to handle the pressure: Advice is sought, problems are analyzed and solutions tried. How similar difficulties were handled is recalled to help define a course of action. Illustration 11 contains a list of commonly used stress control methods these and other students have used.

These students are not unique. They and many others have developed a set of simple but effective methods to manage each day. They know the specifics of managing time, studying effectively and relieving pressure.

Each student's unique system for self-management heightens daily control. *Distress* is defined as "the perception of having lost control." When control is lost, the mental conditions described above appear in various stages. John's panic, resulting from poor organization, moved him to the agony stage. He couldn't concentrate because his mind kept turning to what work remained to be done. As his understanding of concepts and related material diminished, his feelings of failure took hold.

Organizing each day helped these three students manage distress. They were in control of academic responsibilities, and they found time for balance in their lives: membership in campus associations, relaxation, exercise, and fun. Conversations with the three indicated how much they enjoyed their college years. And at the same time, they were laying a foundation for success in the professional school of their choice or in other career directions.

ILLUSTRATION 10. STRESS

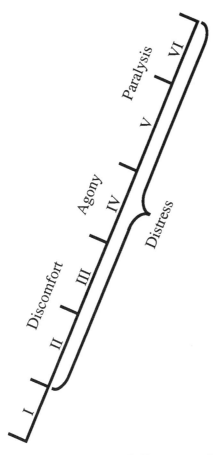

I- Eustress where
concentration
is possible

Regardless of eventual career choice, they knew how to organize to control the pressures likely to be faced. Equally important, they were aware that problems will occur; some can be anticipated and many will demand immediate reaction. All three, moreover, remembered they could solve problems and are stronger persons, as a result.

The beginning step for you is to select a few techniques similar to the ones the three successful students choose. Selection can lead you to a personal approach for self-organization and overall time management of lasting value. The concluding section describes how that approach can be constructed using a few logical techniques.

ILLUSTRATION 11. TECHNIQUES FOR ONE STUDENT
___

Remember to:
1. Plan each study session.
2. Get away from the dorm to study in afternoon and evening.
3. Review lecture notes to spot questions and underline important material.
4. Exercise once each day.
5. Avoid video games until Friday.
6. Avoid bull sessions until Friday.

If you follow this trial process, your own system will emerge and you will use time to achieve your goals. Obviously, success can't be guaranteed, but greater control over each day can, and with it, the opportunity to tap the academic potential that distress might imprison.

Building A Personal Program

Plan for Success / Ellen Kerwin–An Early Beginning / Jane Delio–Determined Not to Slip / John Chandler's Dangerous Approach / Goals and Limits / Three Distinctive Styles / Building a Personal Program / It's Up to You / Bibliography / Appendices

Each person manages time, studies, and controls pressure in a unique way. Through limited experimentation, you can discover which approaches work best for you. Those you choose should help you do three things:

1. Underline the priorities in your life and make saying no to potential time-wasters easier.
2. Develop methods to concentrate intensely while reviewing, preparing for examinations, or completing assignments.
3. Allow you to identify and allocate time to beneficial activities outside your academic work.

Each of the three students used five approaches that soon became time management habits. John Chandler had to develop his under pressure. Ellen and Jane developed their systems in high school and adapted them to fit college course requirements. But even if you didn't get that head start, it's not necessary to go through the kind of ordeal John did before your create your own self-management system.

If you carefully develop a routine to manage your life and habitually follow it, you will systematically move toward academic excellence. You shouldn't spend a great deal of time developing this routine, however. Systems that help people discipline themselves should be simple but effective. The three students and others interviewed are quick to point that out.

Also keep in mind that the techniques that work for others aren't necessarily the ones for you. Create a system suited to your own needs by trying out a few techniques until the best combination appears. With the help of serious fellow students and academic advisors, try this trial process:

1. *Recall* what time management, study, or stress control habits helped you in high school. List them in the space below.

a. _____

b. _____

c. _____

d. _____

e. _____

f. _____

2. *Decide* whether the above habits will satisfy the demands of a preprofessional curriculum, or whether you should add habits of greater self-
   discipline and self-organization.

3. *Select* about five or six approaches from those included in the booklet
   as possible additions to your routine. Ask yourself which approaches
   you might adapt to your current time management, study skill, or
   pressure control habits.

4. *Try* out the approaches as the semester begins, recognizing that you will
   probably eliminate one or two and will personalize the rest.

5. *Assess* their value at the end of every week, sharing what has or hasn't
   worked with fellow students. A brief conference with an advisor may
   also be helpful.

6. *Commit* yourself to as many as five approaches by midterm at the latest.

A list of approaches you will use is a helpful reminder until they become
daily habits. Illustration 12 shows one such list; it was carried on the student's
calendar.

It's Up To You

Just as every personality differs, every time management system differs as well. The individual success stories of Ellen, Jane, and John are proof of this. So remember, whether you keep one, two, or three calendars; whether you study in the economics library or under a friendly sycamore tree, these are not the secrets to success. You are the hero of your own success story, not Ellen's, Jane's or John's. But there are certain key elements that contribute to every happy ending:

1. A *belief* in the value of your goal and your ability to achieve it.

2. A clear *direction* to follow in your pursuit of that goal.

3. The proper *climate* in which to work.

4. *Control* over your work (and play) schedule.

Success demands control, self-discipline, and a clear sense of purpose. Nor are these simply the qualities that make good health professionals; they are also the qualities that make fulfilled and happy people– people who know who they are, who are "masters of their fate." Often the person who has achieved material success through mere good fortune– the sweepstakes winner, for example– is a confused and unhappy person: what fortune gives, fortune can take away, and it very often does. But nothing can take away the knowledge, the self-confidence, and the pride of people who achieve success through their own best efforts.

You will find the *essential techniques* for a successful preprofessional program encapsulated in Illustration 12, under the headings *Belief, Direction, Climate, and Control*. It's up to you to adapt these techniques to your personality and environment.

Remember John Chandler's desperation throughout his wayward freshman year? Remember Ellen Kerwin and Jane Delio's pride and self-confidence, and John's sense of accomplishment after his turnaround?

What will your future be? How will you measure up? The choice is yours. Take control *now* so you can relax later! Be a doer and *make* your dreams come true.

ILLUSTRATION 12

BELIEF

Keep in mind why you want to become a health professional.

Be confident of your ability to achieve your goal.

Consider every success a step along the way to your ultimate goal.

Pat yourself on the back each day by reviewing accomplishments and the techniques that made them possible.

DIRECTION

Identify each semester's goals and list them in order of priority, using the three-ring monitoring technique.

Plan on a Sunday afternoon what you intend to do to achieve your goals in the following week and put your decisions in writing.

Slow down when you feel the pressure mounting and remind yourself of your priorities. What needs to be done now?

ILLUSTRATION 12   (con't.)

CLIMATE

Choose a quiet, out-of-the-way place to study where you can exert maximum concentration for a specific block of time.

Avoid distractions; honestly tell those who interrupt you when studying that you can't talk now.

Set aside a specific block of time to relax and enjoy yourself.

CONTROL

Establish a routine to be followed throughout the semester based on a three-ring monitoring technique.

Keep a weekly calendar (See example in Illustration 3).

Organize files for each subject and keep notes, assignments, tests, and other materials in each file. (Different colored files make identification easier).

Set deadlines for finishing major projects well ahead of schedule to give time for polishing and reviewing, and plan your calendar accordingly.

Break down major tasks into a series of small achievable subgoals.

Prepare a list of each subgoal and keep this list with you at all times.

Finish each subgoal in periods of time set aside each day.

Bibliography

On Study Skills

Johnson, Marcia K., Sally P. Springer and Sarah Hall Sternglanz. *How to Succeed in College.* Los Altos, CA: William Kauffmann, Inc., 1980.

Paul, Walter. *How to Study in College.* Boston: Houghton Mifflin, Co., 1974.

Rowntree, Derek. *Learn How to Study.* New York: Charles Scribner's Sons, 1983.

On Managing Time

MacKenzie, R. Alec. *The Time Trap.* New York: McGraw-Hill, 1972.

Rutherford, Robert. *Just in Time.* New York: John Wiley & Sons, Inc., 1981.

On Handling Pressure

Glasser, William. *Positive Addiction.* New York: Harper & Row, 1976.

Myers, Irma. *Why You Feel Down and What You Can Do About It.* New York: Charles Scribner's Sons, 1982.

Selye, Hans. *Stress Without Distress.* Philadelphia Lippincott, 1974.

On Career Planning

Bolles, Richard N. *What Color is Your Parachute?* Berkeley, CA: Ten Speed Press, 1981.

Bolles, Richard N. *The Three Boxes of Life and How to Get Out of Them.* Berkeley, CA: Ten Speed Press, 1979.

Appendices

1. Effective Techniques
   - Study Skills
   - Examination Preparation
   - Assignment Preparation
   - Assignment Completion
2. Where to Find Help
3. How to Apply to a Professional School

APPENDIX 1. EFFECTIVE TECHNIQUES

Study Skills

1. Reading excellence
   a. Understand that the level of difficulty will vary as will your reading speed.
   b. Recognize that your pace will be slowed down by new terms that should be defined.
   c. Realize different reading purposes: Consider the difference between reading a novel, a chemistry or economics chapter, or mathematics problems.
   d. Choose an appropriate pace and system, such as:
      - rapid skimming to obtain a sense of format and a book's value
      - rapid reading to grasp main points quickly, especially when reading light fiction for pleasure
      - normal speed for understanding text material, outlining, summarizing, and preparing to answer questions
      - careful speed to evaluate or criticize, understand new and difficult material, and solve problems
   e. Concentrate on each reading assignment, determine the most effective rate and what additional activities are appropriate, such as:
      - defining new terms
      - highlighting portions of the text or other material
      - outlining certain material
      - solving problems or answering questions

f. Time yourself to find out how long various kinds of material will take to read and set aside enough time.

g. Become aware of how authors help you to master material through:
- tables of contents
- chapter headings and divisions
- paragraph organization, especially topic sentences
- signal words such as *first, most important, consequently*
- graphs, tables, charts

h. Put material in your own words, develop questions to test understanding, and look for examples from your own experience to illustrate points.

(On many college campuses, you can enroll in a speed reading course. Student service offices along with private organizations sponsor them. You will learn how to increase both speed and comprehension.)

2. Memorizing
   a. Focus on formulas that can be applied to a variety of problems.
   b. Develop a way of remembering items in a logical sequence.
   c. Try to visualize material and then write down key points as a way of testing your understanding.
   d. Memorize entire selections through constant repetition until an entire poem or speech can be repeated without error.
   e. Use index cards with questions on one side and answers on another when preparing to master material.

3. Material Organization
   a. Keep all material for each course in a separate folder or notebook.
   b. Rewrite or summarize lecture notes shortly after each session.
   c. Highlight key points in your notes using a colored marking pen. You may want to highlight portions of a course text book; highlighting alone won't help you master the material. When combined with preparing your own study notes, the highlighting is more effective.
   d. Put all material for each assignment on paper together in one location; doing this you spend less time organizing each time you return to work on the project.
   e. Learn how to operate at least one word processing program you can use for all written assignments. On many campuses, you will find computers to use in residence halls, computer laboratories, college department offices and student service offices. Consult advisors, instructors and

bulletin boards for information on where computers are available for student use.
4. Concentration
   a. Find one location, where seating is solid and lighting sufficient, for serious comfortable study and use it regularly.
   b. Beware of noise and distractions, especially when working on demanding or detail-filled material.
   c. Put distracting objects out of your line of vision.
   d. Set goals for each study session and challenge yourself to improve upon them.
   e. Assemble what you need to finish assignments ahead of time to decrease tendencies to self-interruption.
   f. Begin immediately, working through lack of inspiration or enthusiasm until a momentum begins to build.

Examination Preparation
1. Review how you prepared for examinations in high school, selecting the methods that seemed to work best.
2. Be sure you know what will be tested, and in what way, before you begin studying.
3. Prepare for each examination well in advance, ideally at each study session by noting how you might be tested on points being covered.
4. Review old material as you learn new items and prepare lists and outlines easily examined.
5. Set aside two or three review sessions when all material will be examined; these reviews can be done alone or with a small group of students.
6. Challenge yourself by completing problems or writing essay answers in the same period of time you will be given during the examination.

Assignment Completion
1. Be sure you already understand what is expected.
2. Check with the instructor if you have an idea that might not fall exactly within the guidelines.
3. Set aside time well in advance to begin outlining the assignment, gathering material and preparing the first draft.
4. Use a personal computer to collect information and edit your work. Locate computers available for general student use.
5. Follow accepted format and reference rules.
6. Check and recheck for spelling and punctuation as well as overall organization and clarity.
7. Learn from instructor comments where improvements are needed.

APPENDIX 2. WHERE TO FIND HELP

At *your college library* if you need:

- Guidance on how to use the card catalogue or computer system.
- Counseling on term papers or research projects
- Suggestions on how to locate special material

In *your college administration office* when information on the following becomes important:

- Locating your academic advisor and/or health professions advisor
- Checking on course requirements
- Finding tutorial assistance in a course
- Psychological counseling center
- Reading and study skills center

At *the health center* for physical health problems, counseling and therapy, mental health.

Through *student services* for specialized assistance regarding:

- Financial aid
- Part-time employment
- Counseling
- Special workshops on study skill development, time management, and general self-development
- Career planning

With *recreation services* for:

- Participation in sports programs
- Exercise and fitness programs

With *advisors, student services, and college offices* for:

- Computers available for students
- Course to learn how to operate a computer and both word processing and spread sheet programs

APPENDIX 3. HOW TO APPLY TO A PROFESSIONAL SCHOOL

If you decide to apply for graduate study or enter a professional school, you should begin the selection and application process during your junior year.

1. *Determining* the type of professional school is the first step. Consult with your academic advisor and/or health professional advisor, with graduate students in your area of interest, or with the campus career placement office for information. Then begin to collect catalogues, national service applications and individual applications, identifying the most attractive features of three to five. While selection criteria will differ depending upon the field, generally look for the following:

   - national status of the graduate program

   - comprehensiveness of the program and quality of laboratory and research facilities

   - employment options and success of recent graduates

   - location and other attractive features

   - financial aid resources

2. *Preparing* for entrance examinations is next. You may be required to take general tests such as the Miller Analogies or ones designed for professional schools such as the Medical College Admissions Test (MCAT), DAT, and OCAT. Advisors who specialize in counseling prehealth and prelaw students can suggest appropriate ways to prepare for these major screening procedures.

3. Applying to schools is the final task. Completing application forms, obtaining letters of recommendation, and interviewing are part of this process. Advisors and placement officers on your campus can be particularly helpful as you review all of your application material. You could be admitted to one, several, or none of your first choices. Do not be discouraged if you are turned down; often there are reasons for this which have nothing to do with your personal or academic qualifications. Just turn your attention to other institutions that may be better suited to your needs. As a part of your application, you can also request financial assistance such as fellowships or graduate assistantships. The ability of institutions to meet your financial needs will often be a determining factor in deciding where to attend.

Notes

Notes

Notes

NAAHP PUBLICATIONS

STRATEGY FOR SUCCESS

Written and edited by a committee of experienced health professions advisors from across the country, **STRATEGY FOR SUCCESS: A Handbook for Prehealth Students** addresses questions commonly asked by students interested in health careers:

What should I know about health professional careers?
How do I become a health professional?
Which profession should I enter?
What undergraduate courses should I take?
When do I take my admissions exam?
What are letters of evaluation?
What do I include in my applications?
How do I finance my education?

If you are seriously interested in a health professional career, **STRATEGY FOR SUCCESS: A Handbook for Prehealth Students** is an invaluable reference guide. Used as a supplement to your undergraduate health professions advising office, this handbook will help ready you for all of the steps leading to your health professional education.

STRATEGY FOR SUCCESS Monographs

You may wish for more specific and detailed information about career opportunities, planning your program of study, the application, selection factors, and more. What else do you need to know if you are a pre-medical student? A pre-dental student? A pre-veterinary student? A pre-optometry student? A pre-pharmacy student?

Monographs are now available to answer these specific questions for the fields of medicine (allopathic, osteopathic, podiatric), dentistry, optometry, veterinary medicine, and pharmacy. Utilized in conjunction with your prehealth advising office and **Strategy for Success**, these monographs can help you to prepare for a career in your area of interest.

- **ORDER FORM** -

Please forward:

_____ copy/ies of **Strategy for Success** at $9.95/copy, plus $1.50/copy for postage and handling
_____ copy/ies of **Supplement I - Medicine** at $5.95/copy, plus $1.00/copy for postage and handling
_____ copy/ies of **Supplement II - Dentistry** at $5.95/copy, plus $1.00/copy for postage and handling
_____ copy/ies of **Supplement III - Optometry** at $5.95/copy, plus $1.00/copy for postage and handling
_____ copy/ies of **Supplement IV - Veterinary Medicine** at $5.95/copy, plus $1.00/copy for postage and handling
_____ copy/ies of **Supplement V - Pharmacy** at $3.95/copy, plus $1.00/copy for postage and handling

Name _____
Address _____
City _____ State _____ Zip _____

Please return a copy of this form with your remittance. Make check or money order payable to NAAHP, Inc. No cash, please. Quantity discounts are available upon request. Allow 4 to 6 weeks for delivery. **ALL SALES ARE FINAL.**

Please check:

___ Remittance enclosed
___ VISA ___ MasterCard #_____ Exp. Date _____

Please remit to: **NAAHP, PO Box 5017-A, Champaign, IL 61825**   Phone: **217/333-0090**

Notes

NAAHP PUBLICATIONS

STRATEGY FOR SUCCESS

Written and edited by a committee of experienced health professions advisors from across the country, **STRATEGY FOR SUCCESS: A Handbook for Prehealth Students** addresses questions commonly asked by students interested in health careers:

What should I know about health professional careers?

How do I become a health professional?

Which profession should I enter?

What undergraduate courses should I take?

When do I take my admissions exam?

What are letters of evaluation?

What do I include in my applications?

How do I finance my education?

If you are seriously interested in a health professional career, **STRATEGY FOR SUCCESS: A Handbook for Prehealth Students** is an invaluable reference guide. Used as a supplement to your undergraduate health professions advising office, this handbook will help ready you for all of the steps leading to your health professional education.

STRATEGY FOR SUCCESS Monographs

You may wish for more specific and detailed information about career opportunities, planning your program of study, the application, selection factors, and more. What else do you need to know if you are a pre-medical student? A pre-dental student? A pre-veterinary student? A pre-optometry student? A pre-pharmacy student?

Monographs are now available to answer these specific questions for the fields of medicine (allopathic, osteopathic, podiatric), dentistry, optometry, veterinary medicine, and pharmacy. Utilized in conjunction with your prehealth advising office and **Strategy for Success**, these monographs can help you to prepare for a career in your area of interest.

- **ORDER FORM** -

Please forward:

_____ copy/ies of **Strategy for Success** at $9.95/copy, plus $1.50/copy for postage and handling
_____ copy/ies of **Supplement I - Medicine** at $5.95/copy, plus $1.00/copy for postage and handling
_____ copy/ies of **Supplement II - Dentistry** at $5.95/copy, plus $1.00/copy for postage and handling
_____ copy/ies of **Supplement III - Optometry** at $5.95/copy, plus $1.00/copy for postage and handling
_____ copy/ies of **Supplement IV - Veterinary Medicine** at $5.95/copy, plus $1.00/copy for postage and handling
_____ copy/ies of **Supplement V - Pharmacy** at $3.95/copy, plus $1.00/copy for postage and handling

Name _____

Address _____

City _____ State _____ Zip _____

Please return a copy of this form with your remittance. Make check or money order payable to NAAHP, Inc. No cash, please. Quantity discounts are available upon request. Allow 4 to 6 weeks for delivery. **ALL SALES ARE FINAL.**

Please check:

___ Remittance enclosed

___ VISA ___ MasterCard #_____ Exp. Date _____

Please remit to: **NAAHP, PO Box 5017-A, Champaign, IL 61825** Phone: **217/333-0090**